Space and Dream

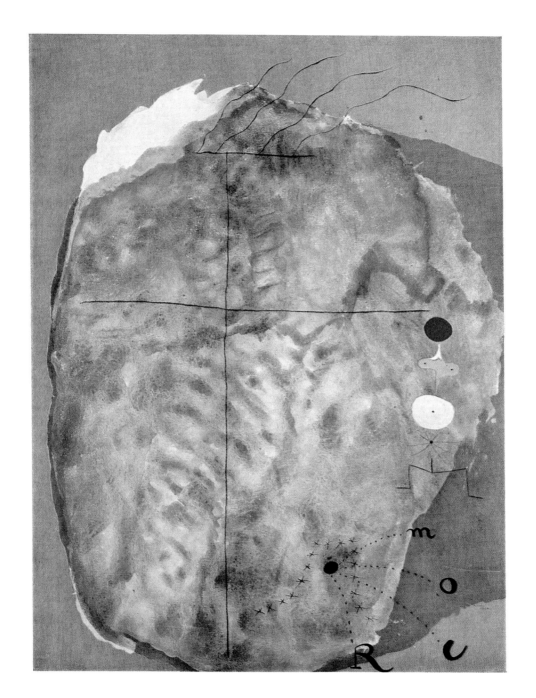

ROBERT GOLDWATER

# Space and Dream

Walker and Company, New York

Frontispiece: Joan Miró. *Amour*. 1926. Oil, 57½ × 44⅞ in. Wallraf-Richartz-Museum, Cologne

PUBLISHED BY WALKER AND COMPANY,
A DIVISION OF THE WALKER PUBLISHING COMPANY, INC.,
IN ASSOCIATION WITH
M. KNOEDLER & CO. INC., NEW YORK.

JUL 2 4 1978

4

# Acknowledgements

*The Publisher and M. Knoedler and Company wish to express gratitude to Dr. Gert von der Osten and Dr. Horst Keller, both of the Wallraf-Richartz-Museum, Cologne, for permission to use the theme of an exhibition they organized there in 1965. Special thanks are due to Dr. Werner Rusche for his help in the preliminary stages of research. It is also a pleasure to thank the individuals and museums listed below who have permitted us to reproduce works from their collections. Almost all of the works reproduced were generously loaned to M. Knoedler and Company for the exhibition held from December 5 through December 29, 1967, and for this we are deeply grateful.*

# List of Lenders

Baltimore Museum of Art; Mr. and Mrs. Raymond J. Braun; Mr. and Mrs. Daniel Brustlein; André Cuvelier; B. H. Friedman; Gorky Estate; The Solomon R. Guggenheim Museum, New York; Michel Guy; Mr. and Mrs. Thomas B. Hess; The Joseph H. Hirshhorn Collection; Philip Isles; Mrs. T. Catesby Jones; Mr. and Mrs. Henry T. Kneeland; Julien Levy; Mrs. Barnett Malbin; Pierre Matisse Gallery; Mr. and Mrs. John de Menil; Munson-Williams-Proctor Institute, Utica; The Museum of Modern Art, New York; Vicomtesse de Noailles; Philadelphia Museum of Art; Mr. and Mrs. Stanley Resor, Jr.; Governor Nelson A. Rockefeller; Dr. and Mrs. Israel Rosen; Mr. and Mrs. Daniel Saidenberg; San Francisco Museum of Art; F. C. Schang; Mr. and Mrs. Joseph Slifka; James Thrall Soby; Mrs. Edward Steichen; Wadsworth Atheneum, Hartford; Wallraf-Richartz-Museum, Cologne; Mrs. Paul Lester Wiener

A number of fundamental concerns appear with surprising frequency in the writings of artists during the years from 1920 to 1940. This period that followed the war and was under the artistic domination of early Cubism witnessed styles that were far from uniform. A dispersed Cubism, Surrealism, various directions of abstraction, and symbolism developed side by side, and though these styles of aesthetic thought seem to have little in common, in many ways the artists' own words appear to belie the fragmentation of these simultaneous developments.

Artists' writings do not, of course, tell the whole story of their preoccupations; these are embodied nowhere but in the works themselves, and revealed to us only if we know how to look at these works. But artists' words are nonetheless true if partial indicators, particularly when they are repetitions of recurrent themes. When painters and sculptors of very different tendencies—artists whose obvious forms and ostensible subjects vary widely, and whose "styles" have little in common—employ the same words to convey concepts that, at a minimum, are closely related, it behooves us to take notice. What are these words and concepts that recur with such frequency and insistence? Space, movement, dream, constellation, and the cosmic: these terms seem to formulate the central concerns of much artistic thinking in the period between the two wars. They appear in the letters, the journals, and the poetic and the didactic essays of artists throughout Europe. And if these ideas are general, if they are mentioned with almost obsessive frequency by artists of contrasting styles, it must be due to the presence of pervading themes that override the conventional historical categories of school and nation.

Space and dream, the cosmic, constellations—such references seem at first glance to have little to do with the visually self-reliant syntax of modern art. Taken literally (or what is perhaps the same, literarily) they are more appropriate to the romantic painting of an earlier century. They suggest landscape and sky, lonely coasts and clouds, the smallness of man and the infinity of nature, moral or mystical allegories, paintings of homiletic mood that may range from Constable to Cole, or from Friedrich to Fuseli. They are lyric terms that hardly bring to mind the analytic development of twentieth century art, its continuing elaboration of pictorial vocabulary, its nuances of structure and modulation of color, its concern for the autonomous reality of the picture plane, and its denial of illusion. Simultaneously both too dependent upon nature and too subjective, these terms seem altogether opposed to the continuing refinement of pictorial means and to the reduction and fragmentation that mark the developments from Cézanne and Seurat through Cubism into geometric and informal abstraction. Such romantic concepts are a long way—or at least so it would appear—from a preoccupation with purely visual structure built from elements themselves increasingly pure, as well as from any goal of self-sufficient plastic compositions. Indeed they contradict it, and rèinstate the traditional alloys—narrative, sentiment, emotion and myth—whose use (or at least whose abuse) the general trend of painting and sculpture in our century had earlier renounced.

If, instead of space and dream (movement and constellations), one says the space of dreams, or perhaps dream-space, the image at once seems to become clearer, and the issue less sharply drawn. For this contraction summons up Surrealism and its infinitely receding spaces that form the landscapes of our dreams: the plains, the deserts and the sea-floors of Tanguy and of Dali. It also recalls the more or less explicit Freudian iconography of the images that inhabit, or are scattered upon, these flat expanses; of Tanguy's amorphic-biomorphic forms, both alive and lost against their backgrounds, more haunting—perhaps because more uniform and more indefinite—than the carefully rendered depictions of Dali's "handmade photographs" with their explicitly erotic double images designed to transcribe the simultaneous presence of a manifest and latent content. But to circumscribe dream and space in this way, to limit their significance to what Masson called "the naturalism of Surrealism," would be to misread both their importance and their pervasive role. For one thing, Dali's use of what he called the "paranoiac-critical method" by which he was, he said, able to exert conscious control over the impulses of his unconscious, ordering rather than recording them, was hardly typical. Much earlier the Surrealists had granted omnipotence to the dream as an article of faith and had practiced ways of setting it down as far as possible unaltered. "I believe," said Breton, "in the future resolution of these two states, so contradictory in appearance—dream and reality—into a kind of absolute reality, of *surreality*, if one may call it so."[1] Therefore Surrealism, as a school, intervened and interrupted the analytic development from Cubism to geometrical abstraction, and played a role in calling upon other than conscious sources in the creation of art, and in reintroducing ambiguous and "literary" meanings. But Surrealism was not alone in this, nor was it even a precursor, although it elaborated a theoretical position. Such impulses were much more widely spread, more general, and largely independent of Surrealism. They are to be found not only in representational art, but in various kinds of abstraction too, and in Germany, Switzerland and Russia as well as in France. Less analyzed, therefore perhaps less labored and so also perhaps less obvious, they are nevertheless fundamental to a wide variety of painting and sculpture in this period.

"The evolution of traditional painting towards concrete art, from Cézanne to the Cubists, has often been explained and these historical explanations have confused the problem," wrote Jean Arp. "Suddenly, 'according to the laws of chance,' towards 1914, the human spirit underwent a transformation."[2] These sentences refer to Arp's own art (to which we will return) and to the techniques and attitudes of Dada, but they might well describe the spirit of de Chirico's metaphysical painting, contemporary with Dada and an influential forerunner of Surrealism. His pictures embody the contradictory world of dreams. Not only do many of them, like the famous *Melancholy and Mystery of a Street* (1914), portray empty spaces, distant horizons, and unreal perspectives, all rendered with a stillness of nostalgic mood, but their elements are brought together in a calm denial of the ordinary roles of transcription and realistic logic, a denial which removes them into the realm of the visionary. De Chirico's unexpected juxtapositions, his exaggerations and reversals of the usual, are documentations of a world that has its own unreasonable coherence. It is not for nothing that mystery, dream, seer and infinite seem appropriately descriptive in the titles of his works. "For a work of art to be truly immortal," he wrote at the time he first conceived the mode of these pictures, "it must completely go beyond the limits of the human; common sense and logic will fail. In this manner it will approach the dream and the mentality of childhood."[3] For this ability to evolve the marvelous, to make the physically impossible psychologically convincing, de Chirico was celebrated by André Breton and the Surrealists, who saw in him "the great exponent of the dream" and their own immediate ancestor—and not only in his effects, but in his method of creation as well. His works are not the unreasonable products of calculation and reason, nor even (like some later creations of the unconscious) of the pragmatic use of associational suggestion; they were created without reflection or adjustment. As James Thrall Soby has described it, de Chirico "relied on inner inspiration to furnish him more or less complete visions, which he then ecstatically transferred to canvas."[4] Thus, despite its complication and detail, de Chirico's dream world, unlike some others that were to follow, is without either cleverness or humor, and has the fascination and the weight of the totally serious.

Both *The Scholar's Playthings* and *Grand Metaphysical Interior* of 1917 are late examples of *pittura metafisica*. The great expanses of the earlier more innocent visions of nostalgia and melancholy with their empty Italianate squares and pseudoheroic statues, their Mediterranean skies and flatly classicizing architectural surfaces, are here replaced by a more programmatic structure. As Soby has noted, their tight construction and the intricate rhythm of their angled planes suggest that de Chirico was aware of Picasso's late Cubist compositions. They are "marked by a more conscious poetic program" than the earlier works.[5] The juxtaposition of barriers, the perspective distortions, and the deliberately startling contrasts of color are matched by the clashing elements of iconography. The almost brutal intrusion of the doubly imaginary distance in the landscape on the easel, which calls into question all the other perspective realities, poses a philosophic problem. These paintings are thus more intellectual and less "visionary" than some of the earlier works. Yet as Soby indicates, they "summarize the ideological premise and vocabulary of *pittura metafisica*," and they moreover contain many elements that were to have an important influence upon later imaginative painting.

As a protagonist of dreams *avant la lettre*, de Chirico was hailed by the Surrealists, and Breton's *Le Surréalisme et la Peinture* of 1928 paid him ample tribute. But his role was a larger one: his world had a profound influence on painters formally allied to Surrealism; although each had his own province, they all accepted it as native country. By 1925, before he came to Paris, Dali was aware of *pittura metafisica*, and after he joined the group in Paris his paintings of the thirties "adopted many of the familiar implements of the Italian painter," especially his long perspectives and his empty spaces.[6] But Dali's precision of rendering ("handmade photography"), his increasing insistence on the obvious genitalial references "hidden" within his academically modeled nudes and objects, his too symbolic paraphernalia of tables and crutches, gave his pictures a peculiar literalness. Such works as *The Persistence of Memory* (1931) (which recalls the Böcklin silences that de Chirico admired but did not copy) are scholastic parsings of a foreign language, learned references to a vocabulary of dreams rather than poetic evocations of mood and feeling. In the end these are not dreams, but merely their diagrams.

Magritte's literalness is of a different, pleasanter sort. His works are more often the ironic observation of a world of magic transformations than memories from within that world itself. They are assemblages, less metaphysical than epistemological, whose separate parts when seen together inform us that the reality we casually accept is only in the mind's eye—or the eye's mind. "Like de Chirico before him, Magritte is fond of . . . the ambiguity between indoor and outdoor setting, which a window can evoke."[7] As Magritte said of a picture called *The Human Condition I* (1934),

> . . . the tree represented in the picture displaced the tree situated behind it, outside the room. For the spectator it was simultaneously inside the room, in the picture, and outside, in the real landscape, in thought. Which is how we see the world, namely, outside of us, though having only one representation of it within us.[8]

Magritte is telling us that the world is surely a dream; but generally his witty, convincing exposition has about it a philosopher's logic: it is essential to this explanation that the world continue to look as before. Only rarely, as in *The False Mirror* (1928), does Magritte create an image of such fused simplicity that inner and outer worlds merge into an unlocalized floating vision that becomes the dream itself.

A more profound affinity with de Chirico is embodied in the gently disturbing mood of Yves Tanguy's beach and seascapes. Tanguy has himself acknowledged the inspiration and described the revelation produced in him by the sudden discovery of de Chirico's art. Not only was de Chirico's perspective central to all of Tanguy's work, but the very manner in which he made it his own matched the older painter's process of creation. For like de Chirico, whose very early Mediterranean impressions counted for so much, Tanguy fused the memories of childhood with those of art, recalling the menhirs, the beaches, and the foggy skies of his native Brittany. Out of these, out of the Italian painter's depths and empy spaces, and out of the subconscious imagery the Surrealists taught him to wel-

Jean Arp. *Shirt Front and Fork*. 1922. Painted wood, 22 × 27½ in. Mr. and Mrs. George Heard Hamilton

come, Tanguy created a very personal world of dreams, recognizably his, haunting to others. Thus without a specific Freudian iconography, but with an awareness of the pervasive implications of simple organic shapes and creatures, Tanguy achieved that subconscious communication that was the Surrealists' goal.

Max Ernst's *Equivocal Woman* (1925) is evidence that he too came under de Chirico's spell. But Ernst is a complicated and various artist (and a learned one) who adapted many visual and theoretical sources to the uses of his own particular dream world. Among the most significant influences were the German romantic painters (especially C. D. Friedrich) and poets—also important for his friend Hans (Jean) Arp—and the Dada ideas of the "laws of chance." Ernst's *collage* novel (*La Femme 100 Têtes*, 1929) and *frottage* drawings and paintings only rarely employ the better known Surrealist symbols, although his imagery can be even more directly erotic. Some of his landscapes, such as those of the *Forest* series, appear at first sight to recall the mood of his German predecessors, but it is quickly apparent that any sentimental naturalism has been replaced by a macabre and even sadistic vision of doom. Many of Ernst's paintings are composed against the open space of dreams (*Monument to the Birds*, 1927, has an unmatched symbolic power), and there is a series of suns and seas that recall the heavenly microcosms of his more abstract and philosophic, and nonSurrealist, contemporaries: Kandinsky, Klee and the Constructivists. But though he willingly employs disturbing anomalies of scale (and of context), Ernst never loses his strong sense of picture surface and material.

Ernst's method of calling into being his imaginative surprises is the chief unifying element of his visions, which he has said, with characteristic (ironic?) immodesty, "vibrate with the incongruous and irrational qualities generally attributed to dreams, although artists know they are the original breath of reality."[9] This is the method of *frottage*, discovered by Ernst in 1925, which "revealed itself as the exact equivalent of [the] automatic writing" practiced by the Surrealist poets.[10] (In fact, it was André Masson who came the closest to transferring this method of pure subconscious impulse to visual art. His violent drawings and sand paintings of the twenties were executed in a state near to trance, out of suggestions given by the material itself.) It consisted in essence of allowing the chance designs made by the grain of wood boards rubbed through paper "to aid the meditative and hallucinatory powers. . . . At random I drop pieces of paper on the floor and then rub them with black lead. By examining closely the drawings thus obtained, I am surprised at the sudden intensification of my visionary capacities."[11] The purpose of such prompting by association (which was later adapted to painting) was twofold: to enlarge "the active part of the mind's hallucinatory faculties," *i.e.*, its unconscious imaginative functioning, and to reduce the artist's conscious involvement and control—at least at the beginning. Waldberg has described *frottage* as a "method in three stages: abandonment, conscience grasp and execution," with these separate phases of creation telescoped as much as possible.[12] By thus seeking "the irritation of his visionary faculties," the artist (to quote Ernst again) "succeeded in attending, simply as a spectator, the birth

Max Ernst. *Equivocal Woman*. 1923. Oil, 51⅜ × 38⅛ in. Mr. and Mrs. Joseph Slifka

of his works." Through this passivity he allowed them to take shape as the accurate projections of an unconscious and therefore heightened reality.

In a sense the ideal expression of space and dream during this whole period is given by the work of Joan Miró. His paintings contain a perfect fusion of the two concepts (which elsewhere are rendered in partial alliance) because for him they are natural modes, never abandoned. He needs neither to recapture them for himself nor reconcile them to each other. And because he himself unhesitatingly inhabits the lyrical world of his paintings, it does not occur to him that he requires either force or calculation, whether of shock or of surprise, to induce us to enter into that world with him.

"He is possibly the most Surrealist of us all," wrote André Breton in 1928.[13] But unlike others, Miró began without the prejudices and handicaps of Cartesian logic and Euclidean vision, and so for him there was really no problem of that "resolution of dream and reality" to which his intellectual friends had to give so much thought and energy. A pictorial composer of intuitive lyrical genius and a consummate craftsman, Miró somehow retained the "mentality of childhood" whose necessity de Chirico invoked and which others had to reconquer if they could. As Jacques Prévert put it, "*L'enfance de l'art prend Miró par la main et l'aide à traverser les rues.*"[14]

For these reasons, Miró's iconography has been only tangentially Freudian. As with Tanguy, erotic references play their part, and double images are unmistakable, but always with characteristic gayety and humor: sex is not a reconquered province, any more than fantasy. Thus, as Ribemont-Dessaignes has written:

> Miró proceeds along an abstractivating road; his forms disengage themselves from the object represented to pursue their own independent plastic life, . . . independent of the changing form and color of the object, and of its particular sentimental meaning, . . . but not of its poetic sense [nor] of the reality of its dream. . . ."[15]

Miró's world is full of signs, numbers, letters, of animals and insects, of figures and parts of figures—heads, feet, lips, eyes and eyelashes, and of fantastic inventions that combine them all. In this he touches upon the programmatic aspects of the dream as conceived by his Surrealist *confrères*. But he is also, as Ribemont-Dessaignes says, the creator of poetic abstractions, and in this he is allied to those other creators of dream worlds, ranging from Arp to Kandinsky and the Constructivists, who proceed less from dream to space than from space to dream.

It is very probable that Miró's "metamorphic figure paintings" with their sudden foreshortenings prompted Picasso to invent the 1928–1929 series of projects for monuments in drawings and paintings, all of which make dramatic use of a drastically deep space.[16] (He probably also knew Tanguy's marine perspectives.) Picasso, who starts with observations from nature, imagined these monuments placed along the Croisette in Cannes, but both they and their spatial setting have been transformed into something fantastic and overwhelming.

*14*

Miró's space is as extraordinary as its population. "The spectacle of the sky overwhelms me," he writes.

> I'm overwhelmed when I see, in an immense sky, the crescent of the moon and the sun. There are, in my pictures, tiny forms in huge empty spaces. Empty spaces, empty horizons, empty plains—everything which is bare has always impressed me. . . . Immobility strikes me. . . . A pebble which is a finite and motionless object suggests to me not only movements, but movements without end. . . . What I am seeking, in fact, is a motionless movement, something equivalent to the eloquence of silence.[17]

("Empty space . . . motionless movement . . . the eloquence of silence," how nearly these phrases describe a work that seems far removed from Miró's ease and innocence: Brancusi's *Bird in Space*. Certainly the sculptor's methods of creation—deliberate, reflective, with a concern for calculated perfection and high finish—were opposed to Miró's. Brancusi's achievement would be called "classic." Yet the fluid shapes of the *Bird* and the *Fish* are not so far from Miró, and Brancusi too invokes space as a kind of incantation.)

The poetry of Miró's pictures is such that we ask no questions as to their means. Perhaps more than any other artist of the period he achieves an imaginary universe that is both near and far, both flat and infinite, a sort of lunar landscape seen simultaneously through telescope and microscope. Roland Penrose writes that:

> Miró has observed with meticulous care the minute paraphenalia of insects, the growth and decay of small flowers, and their seeds, discovering in them the likeness of clouds, volcanoes, suns and planets. . . . He has populated these regions [of space] with his own constellations [and] we find to our surprise that Miró's preoccupation with detail is in fact a means of obtaining some notion of outer space.[18]

It should be emphasized that Miró's poetic universe (his dream of space and silent eloquence) has no further intention than its own imaginary but real existence. Miró has nothing to do with deliberate philosophy. True, he says that in Paris in 1924 and 1925 "I went about a good deal with poets because I thought one must go beyond form to achieve poetry." But just as Miró's iconography of dream is neither literal nor illustrative, and just as his abstraction is neither absolute nor entirely consistent, so his purpose is neither didactic nor symbolic. He is as far from the symbolic microcosms and the mystic idealisms of Klee and Kandinsky as he is from intellectual Surrealism. Seen as an exemplar of a pictorial program, Miró's art is impure (which is very different from being eclectic). Seen from within, it preserves its purity and its own intelligent innocence, confident that no signposts are needed in its poetic universe. For these reasons it stands at the very center of our theme.

"Dreamed plastic works," is how Arp described his early reliefs made of string, cardboard and wood, with their surfaces painted in flat color. They are perhaps dreamed in a double sense. In many of them Arp employs Lautréamont's "convention of the enigmatic

Arshile Gorky. *Untitled.* 1939. 43½ × 31 in. Gorky Estate

encounter" adapted by both Dada (Arp is one of its founders) and Surrealism; he thus brings together unlikely images whose proximity has no reasonable, conscious justification. And these images, or their more abstract counterparts, are seen against a space whose unlimited recession contradicts their immediately tangible construction. Like Miró's, Arp's space is empty and broad, and he composes with the ambiguity of the near and the infinite—a word that appears in several of his titles.

Created inspirationally, Arp's forms, as well as their apparently haphazard encounters, grow out of the Dada principle of chance—submission to the revealing accident. Arp emphasizes the distinction between chance—the single meaningless occurrence— and the "laws of chance"—the hidden but universal rules which govern events we mistakenly call accidental. Nor can reason ever help us to understand them, because it is a human imposition upon nature. It is art's role to identify man with nature:

> Art is a fruit growing out of man like the fruit out of a plant, like the child out of the mother . . . reason tells man to stand above nature and to be the measure of all things. Thus man thinks he is able to live and to create against the laws of nature, and he creates aberrations.[19]

So Arp wrote in *Notes from a Dada Diary*, first published in 1922; while in 1954 he exclaimed: "Reason, that ugly wart, has fallen from man. Logical non-sense has given way to illogical non-sense."

It was with this intention of bathing in the stream of nature that Arp "dreamt" his reliefs of the postwar decade. "Man should be like nature, without measure," he said; and, "A dreamer can make eggs as big as houses." But as Robert Melville has pointed out, Arp's unconscious associations are more formal than symbolic, and his images, never wholly specified, remain ambiguous. A shirt front is also a human mask; a woman, a tree or a cloud; a mirror, a human head; and a navel can equal an eye, or an egg or a sun. This lack of definition permits the union—or the reunion—of many things usually thought to be entirely different and separate; it allows "particular form [to] become universal form, moving according to invisible forces within the cosmic scheme."[20] Space is always an important element for these effects, and there are a number of reliefs (such as *Infinite Amphora*, 1929) that have been described as "relief maps of a poetic cosmogony." These works in particular are related to Arp's lifelong interest in the pre-Socratic philosophers and to "their speculations upon the originative material of things and the coherence of the natural world." But not only these. Carl Einstein spoke of Arp's "neolithic world," and his series of *Constellations* and ambiguous *Configurations* are similar to the allegorical and parallel thinking (logic or illogic) that belongs to that world.

"Constellation" seems to be a natural title for many works of Miró and Arp. It refers to a grouping of basic forms, at once abstract and suggestive, sparsely set out against a space that implies expanse and depth. These essential elements are to be found again in the paintings of Klee and Kandinsky, but with a difference, because they are employed with a deliberate symbolic intention, and something like a philosophy.

That space, and not simply the analytic space of the Cubist tradition (which they see as a thing of the past), is important to both artists is evident enough. Stars, moons and suns often appear in Klee's pictures, and sometimes a shore or desert seems to be described from some high and distant vantage point, implying the intervening sky. In Kandinsky's paintings of this period, abstract as they are, the circular and crescent shapes inevitably suggest heavenly bodies and an immense surrounding space. Yet it is equally clear that, though they may imply emotion at the spectacle of the cosmos, these are not ordinary romantic depictions of awe or melancholy before the vastness of the universe and the smallness of man. There are here neither vistas nor perspectives: Klee's pictures are of miniature size; Kandinsky's, even those that most suggest space, are not much larger, and their elements are relatively large and few.

Kandinsky himself recognized this connection with the older romanticism, which, however, he wanted to transcend: "It is no part of my program to paint with tears, or to make people cry, and I really don't care for sweets, but Romanticism goes far, far beyond tears. Today there is a *Neue Sachlichkeit*; why should there not be a (or the) New Romanticism. . . . The meaning, the content of art is Romanticism, and it is our fault if we mistake a temporal phenomenon for the whole notion. . . ."[21]

But Kandinsky also intended his art to go beyond purely formal abstraction. He was very conscious of picture construction, of how the elements in his compositions lay on the surface or "floated as though in an indeterminate space," according to the play of texture and color; these abstract relationships were of primary importance to him. Though he was convinced that the future belonged to abstract art, he was "distressed when other abstract artists fail to go beyond questions of form."[22] But to go beyond form did not mean to go back to traditional romantic associations; that the circle was, in his words, "a link with the cosmic" did not mean that it should call up sentimental memories of the heavens and a starry sky.

Kandinsky's thinking was much influenced by his reading of German idealist philosophy, of theosophy, and of the Indian philosophers; they had initially been a powerful impetus in determining his adherence to abstraction. Without going into the details of his theories, it can be said that they played an important role in fixing the constituents of his "constellations," their relative placement and their colors. Kandinsky was aware that most viewers would interpret his paintings as cosmic metaphors by simple visual association. For him they were something else, not metaphors, but autonomous microcosms whose structure paralleled the hidden generative forces of the world—the true spiritual reality behind the false reality of appearance. The colors and the shapes are the symbols of these hidden forces and the relationships symbolize their interaction. This does not imply simple philosophic illustration: the picture must function as a microcosm and so convey the feeling of the underlying reality of the macrocosm: "The external matter of art will again recede, and we will have an art of universal content." This is what he means when he says "I should like people to see what is *behind* my art, for this is the

Wassily Kandinsky. *Support-
ed*. 1927. Oil, 31⅛ × 20½ in.
Dr. and Mrs. Israel Rosen

only thing I really care about. . . . Form for me is only a means to an end. . . . I want to capture the inner secrets of form."[23]

Although his solutions were of a very different kind, Paul Klee was concerned with many of these same problems. His imaginary creatures float through space, watched over by heavenly bodies (*Under the Spell of the Stars*, 1921); and these bodies are themselves transformed into partially human faces still surrounded by space (*Physiognomic Lightning*, 1927); or the striped landscape of a sky projects out of itself an amazed head that still partakes of its atmosphere (*Thoughtful*, 1927). Characteristically, Klee's figures are reduced to heads without bodies, since only the imagination is important. Like Miró, he allows one form to lead him on to another, and his punning representations, which mock the seriousness we customarily lend to appearance, give his work its typical irony.

Klee is, in fact, questioning the reality of everyday sensations and their accepted surface, and suggesting that there are many other sorts of worlds possible. These can be reached, as he said, by calling on "those parts of the creative process which are carried on largely in the subconscious while the work is taking form." This search is something other than an individual psychological probing, for in thus letting himself go, the artist comes "nearer to the heart of all creation." Instead of a "finished image of nature" he perceives and can render "its genesis, the only essential thing." "Our pounding heart drives us down, deep down to the primordial underground . . . to live where the central organ of all space-time motion, call it brain or heart of creation as you will, activates all functions."[24] Thus Klee uses his imaginative faculty ("Whether it is called dream, idea, or fancy") to express through pictorial microcosms the inner essence of what he calls "the world in between." This is a world that "children, madmen and savages see into" without effort, prompted by an unconscious vision; it is a world that the artist can approach through his pictorial imagination: "It exists between the worlds our senses can perceive, and I absorb it inwardly to the extent that I can project it outwardly in symbolic correspondence."[25] It is toward this dream of essences that art should tend. In Klee's famous phrase: "Art plays an unconscious game with ultimate things, and achieves them nevertheless."

A new concept of space, and of its direct visual realization in the arts, is of course at the very core of Constructivism. The "Realistic Manifesto" of 1920, in which Gabo and Pevsner summarized their views, stated clearly that "the realization of our perceptions of the world in the forms of space and time is the only aim of our pictorial art."[26] They renounced mass as a sculptural means and attribute, but more than this, they gave up the "descriptive value" of line, and even denied the traditional use of volume. What remained was "depth as the only pictorial and plastic form of space . . . and line as a direction," but line utilized to "affirm depth as the one form of space." This strong definition of an abstract art was anticipated in their own work done before that date, the still figurative heads and busts in metal and plastic which translated the reversals of solid and void already suggested by the facets of Cubist painting into the actuality of three dimensions.

Gabo and Pevsner were not the only Russian sculptors whose imagination was captured by the artistic possibilities of space, and by its philosophic implications—an ambience that also had its importance for Kandinsky. The handling of space is central to Tatlin's early reliefs (which also quite literally expand the ideas of Cubism) and to his later constructions (of which the best known is his design for a monument to the Third International of 1920); as well as to Rodchenko's circular and spherical constructions which seem inspired by planetary movements. Malevich was also fascinated with the expression of space. Some of his compositions were inspired by airplane views, and he was very soon combining the basic Suprematist elements ("supremacy of pure feeling or perception") of 1913–1914 into drawings "expressing the sensation of flight," or "conveying a feeling of universal space."[27]

Constructivism, then, starts with the meaning and experience of space as its primary concern. Whatever materials the Constructivists employ—and they range from the bronze and copper of Pevsner, to the glass and plastic of Gabo, to Moholy-Nagy's experiments with light—space is always the real substance to be given shape. What is less evident is that despite some scientific training none of these artists wish to approach the realization of space as scientists. Certainly the new concepts of physics—the relative emptiness of matter previously thought to be solid, the shape of the universe, and especially the relativity of space and time—influenced their artistic attitudes. But as Gabo and Pevsner repeatedly emphasized, they were not translating mathematical equations. They were poets of space who wanted to make the void directly visible and so to give it an immediate emotional impact. Malevich had already been influenced by mystic ideas from the East (*cf.* his *Suprematist Composition conveying a feeling of a mystic wave from outer space*, 1917) as well as by Western ideas of scientific progress, and such thinking was not alien to the Constructivists. As philosophic idealists who were also artists, they used the tangible as the path to the intangible.

"Science," wrote Pevsner, "puts us in constant relation with objective knowledge and reason, but art has no trace of such knowledge, the more so since it is passion that inspires the artist; it is love, it is pure poetry."[28] "Space," maintained Gabo, "is a concrete element of our vision playing an active role in the structure of an image in a painting or a sculpture."[29] While Pevsner stressed the role that "instinct and intuition" play in artistic creation, Gabo, with rationalist objections to the Surrealist attitude, insisted that there is "no need to undertake remote and distant navigations in the subconscious in order to reveal a world which lies in our immediate vicinity."[30] The space they conceive is neither abstract nor imaginary; neither is it the space of dreams. It is not, however, the space of the surveyor, or even that of the astronomer, although (as with Kandinsky) their images sometimes resemble the artists'. Although made immediately sensible through their work, Constructivist space is based on the underlying realities of space and time.

Paul Klee. *Thoughtful.*
1928. Watercolor, 15½ ×
8½ in. F. C. Schang

Their sculpture, like Mondrian's painting, proposes to make space visible because it reflects the true nature of the universe.

Whether directly in the wake of Constructivism or more independently within the changing mood of the times (to which Constructivism contributed), other sculptors too abandoned massive design and began to compose with a fluid and penetrating space. Lipchitz, who had been working in the Cubist compactness of hard stone, executed his series of "aerial transparencies" (*The Harp Player*, 1928) in which contour alone sufficed to render volume, permitting space to flow through forms now visible from all sides. This is something more radical than the simple piercing of Cubist mass—which Lipchitz had earlier been one of the first to practice—a method further developed by Henry Moore, who adapted it to the organic forms of the thirties (*Carving*, 1935). Picasso's iron-wire constructions of ca. 1929 seem to be three-dimensionally open transpositions of the line and dot drawings that had earlier (1926) illustrated the *Chef d'Oeuvre Inconnu*: both were significant sources for postwar, and particularly American, sculpture. About the same time Gonzalez, influenced by Picasso, evolved his stylized welded-iron figure sculpture (also seminal for developments in the fifties), and put its imaginative spatial qualities at the exceptional service of intense human expression. Gonzalez' work also starts from Cubism, whose suggestions of convex-concave reversals he has, so to speak, taken literally, replacing a solid with a void that is simply outlined. His purpose, he said, was "to project and design in space with the help of new methods, to utilize this space and to construct with it as though one were dealing with a newly acquired material." In this way, as Gonzalez said, "There is a union of real forms with imaginary forms, obtained or suggested by established points or by perforation—and according to the natural law of love, to make them inseparable. . . ."[31] What is not present has the same psychological impact as what is, and thus Gonzalez, like the Surrealists, comments upon the relativity, the constant shifting, and the interpenetration of real and unreal.

Calder's sculpture obviously belongs to our theme of space; but it belongs in an idiosyncratic way that goes beyond his invention of the mobile, important as that is. The suggestions that Calder derived from the ambience of the time are all evident enough: something of the mockery of Dada in his *Circus* (1926–1927) and his first handmade mechanized constructions; the space concept of the Constructivists themselves (and even occasionally their compositional themes, as in the *Universe*, 1934); the fluidly curved forms of Miró and Arp, and perhaps Miró's blacks and reds—the debt here is clear and it is one of his qualities that he accepts it so readily. But Calder made all this entirely his own when he created his mobiles, and not only through his feeling for delicate design and by his engineering sense that hung the finely balanced forms. Close as his work is in many respects to that of friends and contemporaries, it is in one sense defiantly (or humorously) opposed. Where others—including the sculptors—were creating a virtual, artistic space, "real" in being more real than the space of everyday actual experience, Calder made a continuum of the two. "In a constructive sculpture," writes Gabo, "space is not part of the universal space that surrounds the object . . ." (although there are some Gabos where this is clearly not the case).[32] Calder's mobiles, on the contrary, make us aware of relationships inside the space that is our natural habitat; they are part of and within our natural space. As their parts trace designs, forces, and everchanging relationships, we watch with a direct empathic pleasure that almost summons our own action. Because Calder's work, however abstract, possesses this special kind of realism, it conveys its particular feeling of heightened vitality.

These sculptural concerns with space—whether ideal or real, virtual or actual—have little to do with dream; indeed Gabo specifically denies any such connection. But for Alberto Giacometti space and dream are inextricably linked. The union of the two that Giacometti expressed in his work was not dependent on his friendship with the Surrealists; he was never a formal member of the group. His whole manner of conception is anything but programmatic, although *Pointe à l'oeil* (1951) has recognizable Dalian affinities. It is rather that, from childhood on, Giacometti's dreams exercised a compulsive power over his imagination and that as a consequence his conception of reality bore little resemblance to commonly accepted appearance. It is therefore not too much to say that in his work of the thirties, in which space plays a dominant role (different from the role it was to assume in his postwar figure sculpture), space and dream are fused.

Giacometti's work of the mid-twenties did, as he put it, "touch on Cubism," although even then it was strongly symbolic since it employed signs and formal simplifications related to preclassical icons that in their turn expressed mythologies. Many of these references continued in the sculpture of the thirties. But then, as observation became too painful and he was forced to work only from memory, his own "vision of reality" intervened and with it space inevitably interjected itself in order to complete that vision: ". . . a structure, also a sharpness that I saw, a kind of skeleton in space. Figures were never for me a compact mass but like a transparent construction" (*Reclining Woman Who Dreams*, 1929), partially interrupting, but not blocking a spatial continuum.[33]

Again, in what Giacometti described as "cages with open construction inside, executed in wood by a carpenter," space is the primary entity; asserted by the cage, it is the void into which the solids are later introduced. These inserted forms are either unconnected or only barely touch each other, and the intervals of space still control their isolation.

The drama of loneliness, of figures reduced and immobilized by distance, held apart and unaware, has its most poignant rendering in two contrasting works. The famous *Palace at 4 A.M.* (1932-1933) is a skeleton house inhabited by a spinal column within its own private cage, a skeletal bird that flies above it, a statue of a woman against a curtain, and a red object in front of a board. Giacometti has described the circumstances of the emotional crisis in which this ghostly vision was conceived. The spine and the bird derive from immediate events in his existence, but the statue is an image of his mother as she appeared in his earliest memories, and the curtain is an even older recollection; the red object he identifies with himself. But he cannot explain how it is that these images of

Joan Miró. *L'Hirondelle d'Amour*. 1934. Oil, 78½ × 97½ in. Governor Nelson A. Rockefeller

past and present have come together in this way. In *No More Play* (1933), which he described as a "moon landscape," the small contrasting figures are held—isolated and at distance—in two depressions of the expanse of the white marble base. Not facing each other, seemingly standing at random in an immense desert, they are irrevocably divided by the three open tombs between them. Here again, as in the caged trance of the *Palace*, no communication can bridge these distances; there is only silence and solipsistic isolation. Each is a dream of despair.

Much of what has been reviewed here concerning space and dream had as one of its immediate sources opposition to the style and the assumptions—both philosophical and psychological—implicit in Cubism. This revolt was thought out and expressly acknowledged by artists as different as Arp and Gabo, Klee and Mondrian, and even when unexpressed was generally felt. It was as though the painters and sculptors (each in his own way) were refusing the limits that early Cubism had set for itself: on the one hand its minute and rational visual analysis of a small section of a familiar environment—studio interior, still-life or figure; on the other its deliberate reduction of spatial rendering which squeezed objects and intervals between two narrow planes and insistently interposed the reality of paint and canvas between the observer and a supposed illusion. Space and dream were a double rejection of this approach: a rejection of bas-relief in favor of deep and often infinite recession with a compositional rhythm that penetrates the surface (and that in sculpture replaces mass with void); and, just as significant, a rejection of reasoned analysis in favor of profounder irrational impulses whose associational directions are unhesitatingly accepted. The effect of these new tendencies upon those artists who still remained essentially Cubist (most notably Picasso) makes it evident that they were strong and widespread.

Still, the conquests of Cubism could not simply be discarded. Klee and Kandinsky inveighed against its materialism, but it affected their consciousness of design and their conviction that even the transposed symbol of a (metaphysically and psychologically) hidden universe had first of all to be a functioning pictorial object. The evolution of Mondrian and the Constructivists out of Cubism is clear enough, and their most spatially felt works retain its evidence. Arp's insistence on the term *"l'art concret"* to emphasize the materiality of his most abstract works is along similar lines. And an essential element in the impact achieved by the most ardent exponents of deep dream-space is their struggle with that consciousness of the flat existence of the canvas which the Cubists had made unavoidable.

This is indeed the double lineage of the New York school that rises in the forties. It reworks Cubism within an imaginary space whose psychological reality the two preceding decades had taught it; and like its immediate predecessors it trusts the validity of unconscious impulses and the communicative power of apparently inexplicable images. Gorky, indebted to Picasso and Cubism, and to Miró and Matta, arbitrates these two tendencies to create his own style. His brightly colored forms, endowed with unspecified organic and erotic references, are designed to hold the surface, but at the same time these forms are suspended in an unreal space of unknown dimensions. De Kooning, perhaps partly because of Gorky, briefly smooths out his shapes and opens up his space; and Jackson Pollock's early style, however Cubist its flattened composition, is also grounded in symbolic reverie. Later, after 1945, the spreading, simultaneously advancing and receding floating areas found in much of American painting are a reconciliation and a transformation of these tendencies of more than two decades; they are conceived in a space neither flat nor deep, at once expansive and suffused, both impassable and immaterial.

Robert Goldwater

## References

1. André Breton, *Le manifeste du surréalisme*, Paris, 1924, cited in Patrick Waldberg, *Surrealism*, New York, 1965, p. 70.
2. Jean Arp, *Jours éffeuillés*, Paris, 1965, p. 183.
3. Cited by André Breton, *Le surréalisme et la peinture*, Paris, 1965, p. 18. (Original edition, 1928.)
4. James Thrall Soby, *The Early Chirico*, New York, 1941, p. 48.
5. *Ibid.*, p. 76.
6. *Ibid.*, p. 97.
7. James Thrall Soby, *Magritte*, New York, 1965, p. 15.
8. *Ibid.*
9. William S. Lieberman, ed., *Max Ernst*, New York, 1961, p. 18.
10. *Ibid.*, p. 14.
11. *Ibid.*
12. Patrick Waldberg, *Max Ernst*, Paris, 1958, p. 290.
13. Breton, *op. cit.*, p.37.
14. Jacques Prévert and G. Ribemont-Dessaignes, *Joan Miró*, Paris, 1956, p. 47.
15. *Ibid.*, p. 79.
16. Alfred H. Barr, Jr., *Picasso*, New York, 1946, p. 150.
17. Joan Miró, *Je travaille comme un jardinier*, Paris, 1964, pp. 39, 42.
18. Roland Penrose, *Creación en el Espacio de Joan Miró*, Barcelona, 1966, p. 17.
19. Cited in James Thrall Soby, ed., *Arp*, New York, 1958, p. 27.
20. *Ibid.*, p. 21.
21. Will Grohmann, *Kandinsky*, New York, 1958, p. 179.
22. *Ibid.*
23. *Ibid.*
24. Paul Klee, *The Thinking Eye*, New York, 1961, pp. 92–93.
25. Felix Klee, *Paul Klee*, New York, 1962, p. 184.
26. Cited in Naum Gabo, *Gabo: Constructions, Sculpture, Paintings, Drawings, Engravings*, Cambridge, 1957, p. 152.
27. Kasimir Malevich, *The Non-Objective World*, Chicago, 1959, *passim*.
28. Antoine Pevsner, "La science tue la poésie," *XX Siècle*, No. 12, Mai-Juin, 1959, p. 13.
29. Naum Gabo, *Of Divers Arts*, New York, 1962, p. 100.
30. Pevsner, *op. cit.*, p. 14. Naum Gabo, "The Constructive Idea in Art," *Circle*, London, 1957, cited in *Gabo*, 1957, p. 164.
31. New York, The Museum of Modern Art, *Julio Gonzalez*, intro. by A. C. Ritchie, New York, 1956, p. 42.
32. Gabo, *Of Divers Arts*, p. 100.
33. New York, The Museum of Modern Art, *Alberto Giacometti*, intro. by Peter Selz, New York, 1965, p. 35.

Pablo Picasso. *Tête* (*Study for a Monument*). 1929. Oil, 28¾ × 23½ in. Baltimore Museum of Art. Gift of Dexter M. Ferry, Jr., Trustee Corporation of Detroit, Michigan

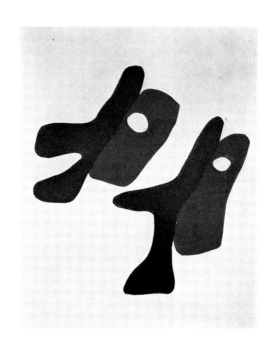

Jean Arp. *Les Deux Sœurs*. 1927. Painted cardboard, 29½ × 23⅝ in. André Cuvelier

Jean Arp. *Lèvres et Glace à Main*. 1927. Painted wood, 22¹³⁄₁₆ × 39⅜ in. André Cuvelier

Jean Arp. *Relief.* 1930. Painted wood, 23½ × 17¾ in.
Mrs. George Henry Warren

Jean Arp. *Variation I Constellation with Five White and Two Black Forms.* 1932. Painted wood, 23⅛ × 29⅛ in. Munson-Williams - Proctor Institute, Utica

Jean Arp. *Configuration*. 1930. Painted wood, 27½ × 33½ in. A. E. Gallatin Collection, Philadelphia Museum of Art

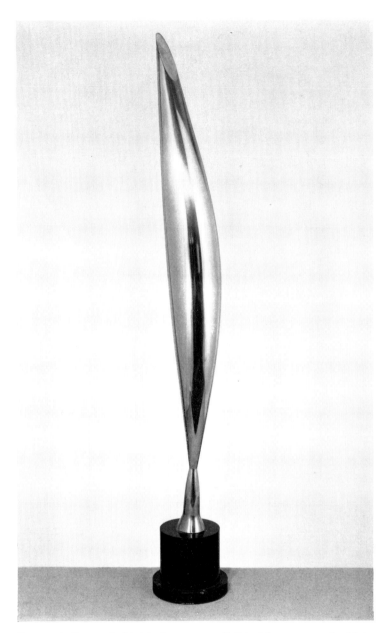

Constantin Brancusi. *Bird in Space*. 1925. Polished bronze, 50¼ in. high; upper base 6⅝ in. high; lower base 41⅛ in. high. Louise and Walter Arensberg Collection, Philadelphia Museum of Art

Constantin Brancusi. *Bird in Space.* 1925. Polished bronze, 53½ in. high; base of two limestones and one wood section, 60½ in. high. Mrs. Edward Steichen

Alexander Calder. *Motorized Mobile*. 1929. Wood and wire, 23 × 24½ in. The Joseph H. Hirshhorn Collection

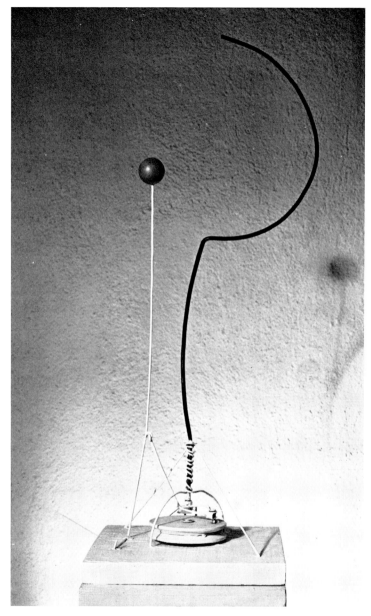

Alexander Calder. *Double Arc and Sphere*. 1932. Wood and wire, 24 in. high. Berkshire Museum, Pittsfield

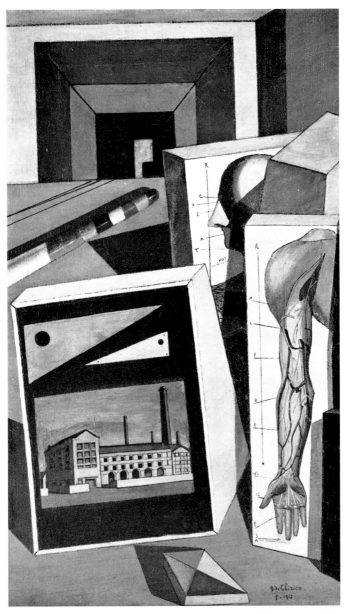

Giorgio de Chirico. *The Scholar's Playthings*. 1917. Oil, 35¼ × 20¼ in.
Courtesy Pierre Matisse Gallery

Giorgio de Chirico. *Grand Metaphysical Interior*. 1917. Oil, 37¾ × 27⅜ in. James Thrall Soby

Salvador Dali. *Accommodations of Desire*. 1929. Oil, 8⅝ × 13¾ in. Mr. and Mrs. Julien Levy

Willem de Kooning. *Untitled*.
1938. Oil, 9½ × 15 in. Mr. and
Mrs. Thomas B. Hess

Willem de Kooning. *Abstract
Still Life*. c. 1938. Oil, 25 × 30 in.
Mr. and Mrs. Daniel Brustlein

Max Ernst. *Forest.* 1927. Oil, 44⅞ × 57½ in. Mr. and Mrs. Joseph Slifka

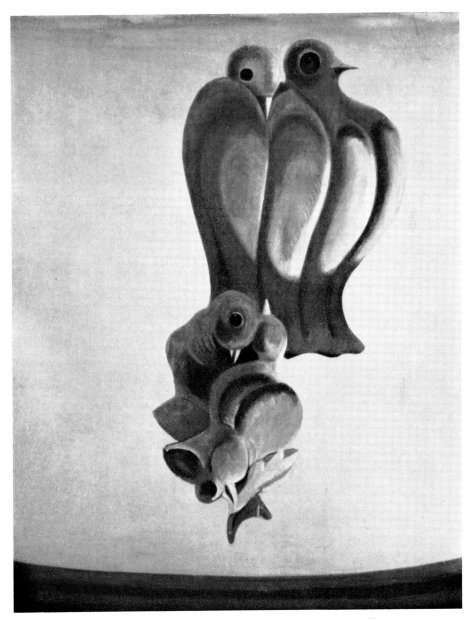

Max Ernst. *Monument to Birds*. 1927. Oil, 64 × 51¼ in. Vicomtesse de Noailles

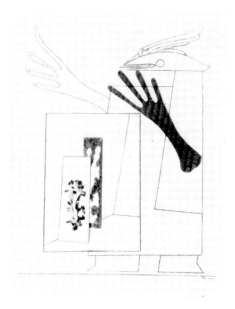

Max Ernst. *Lop Lop Introduces*. 1928. Pasted paper, pencil and crayon, 25⅜ × 19⅝ in. Mr. and Mrs. Julien Levy

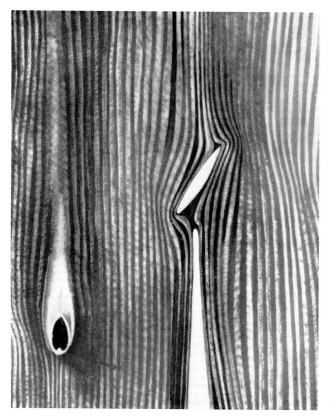

Max Ernst. *Blind Swimmer*. 1934. Oil, 36¼ × 28⅞ in. Mr. and Mrs. Julien Levy

Max Ernst. *La Belle Allemande*. 1935. Bronze, 24 in. high. D. and J. de Menil

Max Ernst. *Gai*. 1935. Bronze, 17½ in. high. Mr. and Mrs. Joseph Slifka

Naum Gabo. *Construction*. 1933. Stone, slate and plastic, 8 × 13½ in. Private collection, New York

Alberto Giacometti. *Man and Woman*. 1928. Bronze, 12 in. high. The Joseph H. Hirshhorn Collection

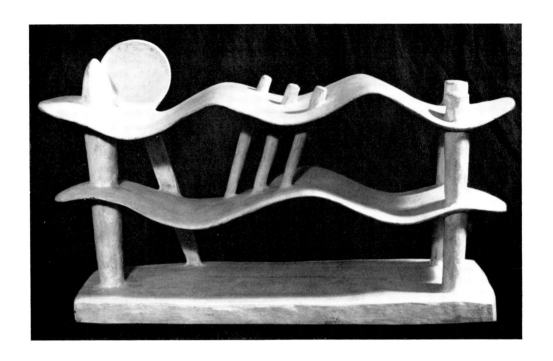

Alberto Giacometti. *Reclining Woman Who Dreams.*
1929. Painted bronze, 9¼ in. high, 16⅝ in. wide,
5 in. deep. The Joseph H. Hirshhorn Collection

Alberto Giacometti. *Standing Man.* 1930. Poly-
chrome plaster, 26 in. high. The Joseph H. Hirshhorn Collection

Alberto Giacometti. *No More Play*. 1933. Marble, wood and bronze, 25 × 17⅝ in. Mr. and Mrs. Julien Levy

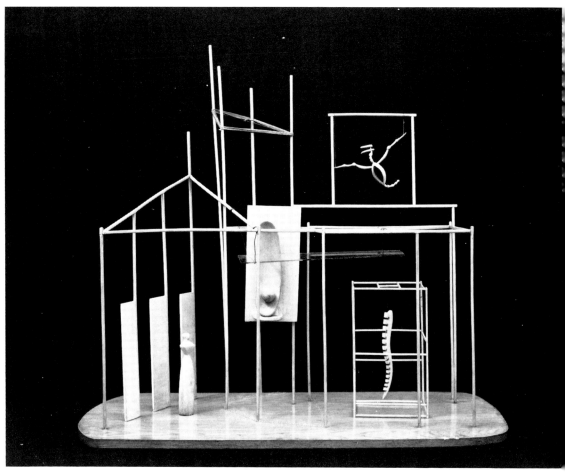

Alberto Giacometti. *The Palace at 4 A.M.* 1932–33. Construction in wood, glass, wire, string, 25 in. high, 28¼ in. wide, 15¾ in. deep. Collection, The Museum of Modern Art, New York. Purchase

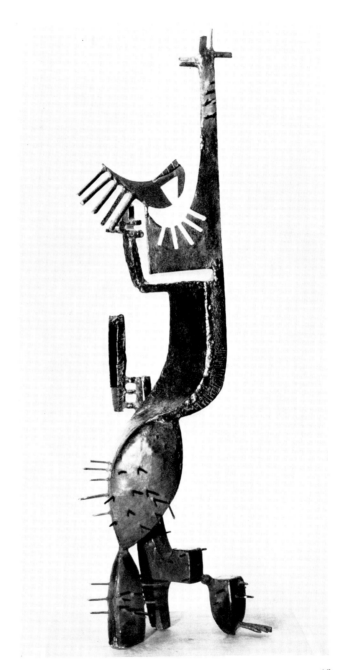

Julio Gonzalez. *Cactus Man II.*
1939. Bronze, 30¾ in. high. Mun-
son - Williams - Proctor Institute,
Utica

Julio Gonzalez. *Head*. 1935? Wrought iron, 17¾ in. high. Collection, The Museum of Modern Art, New York. Purchase

Arshile Gorky. *Garden in Sochi*. 1958–42. Oil, 25 × 29 in. Gorky Estate

Wassily Kandinsky. *Blue Circle No. 242*. 1922. Oil, 42⅞ × 39 in. The Solomon R. Guggenheim Museum, New York

Wassily Kandinsky. *Luminosity*. 1927. Oil, 20½ × 13½ in. Mrs. Barnett Malbin (The Lydia and Harry Lewis Winston Collection)

Wassily Kandinsky. *Brownish*. 1931. Oil on board, 19 × 27½ in. San Francisco Museum of Art. William Gerstle Collection

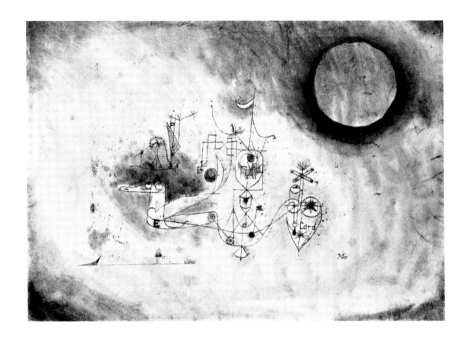

Paul Klee. *Under the Spell of the Stars*. 1921. Oil, watercolor and ink, 12¼ × 17½ in. Private Collection

Paul Klee. *Physiognomic Lightning*. 1927. Watercolor, 10 × 10 in. Mr. and Mrs. Daniel Saidenberg

54

Paul Klee. *Fish Magic*. 1925. Oil, 30½ × 38¾ in. Louise and Walter Arensberg Collection, Philadelphia Museum of Art

Paul Klee. *Twins*. c. 1930. Oil and watercolor on canvas, 23⅞ × 20 in. Mr. and Mrs. Henry T. Kneeland

Paul Klee. *Classic Coast*. 1931. Oil, 31⅞ × 27⅛ in. Mr. and Mrs. Stanley R. Resor

Paul Klee. *Spiral Schrauben Blüten I, V 17*. 1932. Watercolor, 18¾ × 12¼ in.
F. C. Schang

Paul Klee. *Barbarian Sacrifice*. 1932. Watercolor, 24½ × 18½ in. F. C. Schang

Fernand Leger. *Composition with Keys.* 1929. Oil, 36 × 29 in. Mr. and Mrs. Daniel Saidenberg

Fernand Leger. *Composition with Aloes*. 1934–35. Oil, 44⅞ × 57½ in. The Solomon R. Guggenheim Museum, New York

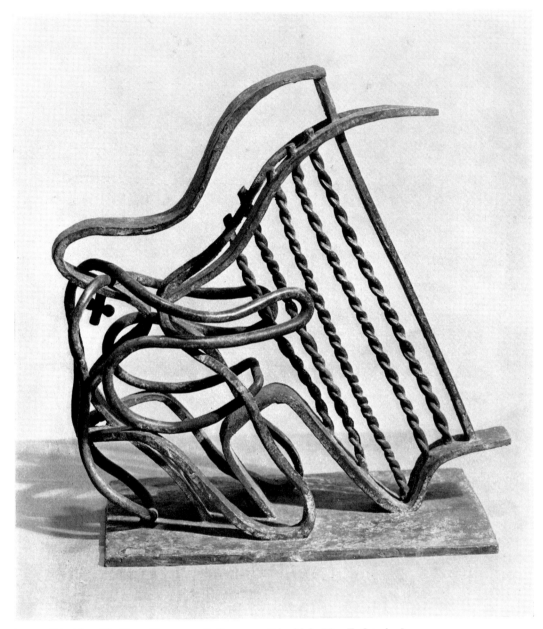

Jacques Lipchitz. *The Harp Player*. 1928. Bronze, 10½ in. high. Mrs. T. Catesby Jones

René Margritte. *The Empty Mask.* 1928. Oil, 52 × 45¾ in. Mr. and Mrs. Raymond J. Braun

René Margritte. *The False Mirror.* 1928. Oil, 21¼ × 31⅞ in. Collection, The Museum of Modern Art, New York. Purchase

Kasimir Malevich. *Suprematist Composition (Airplane Flying)*. 1914. Oil, 22⅞ × 19 in. Collection, The Museum of Modern Art. Purchase

Man Ray. *Composition*. 1929. Oil, 21½ × 29 in. The Joseph H. Hirshhorn Collection

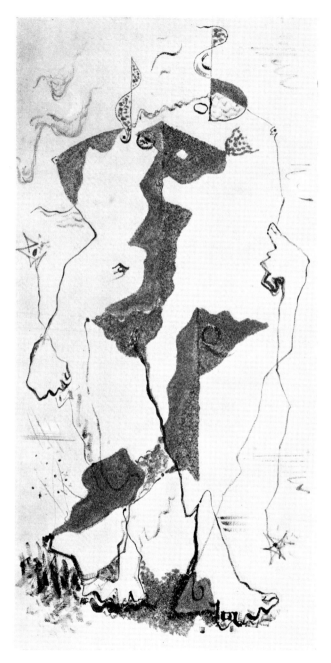

André Masson. *Les Promeneuses.*
1927. Oil and sand, 28¾ × 14½ in.
The Joseph H. Hirshhorn Collection

Matta. *Prescience*. 1959. Oil, 36 × 52 1/16 in. Courtesy Wadsworth Atheneum, Hartford. The Ella Gallup Sumner and Mary Catlin Sumner Collection

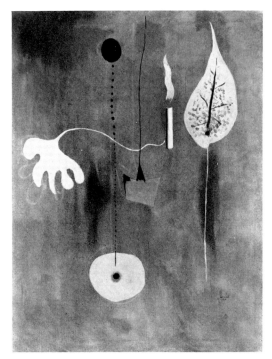

Joan Miró. *The Candle*. 1925. Oil, 45⅞ × 35 in. Mrs.
Paul Lester Wiener

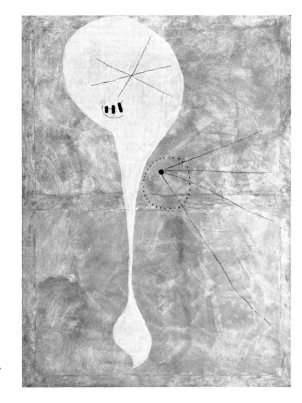

Joan Miró. *Personnage*. 1925. Oil, 51¼ × 38⅛ in. The
Solomon R. Guggenheim Museum, New York

*68*

Joan Miró. *Landscape*. 1927. Oil, 51¼ × 76¾ in. The Solomon R. Guggenheim Museum, New York

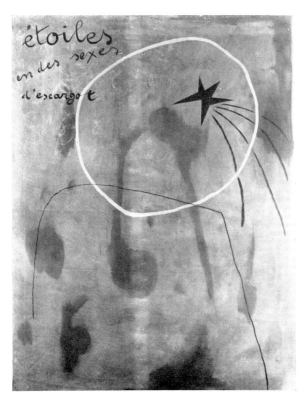

Joan Miró. *Étoiles en des sexes d'escargot.* 1925. Oil, 51¼ ×
38½ in. Pierre Matisse Gallery

Joan Miró. *Painting (Fratellini).* 1927. Oil, 51 × 38 in. A. E.
Gallatin Collection, Philadelphia Museum of Art

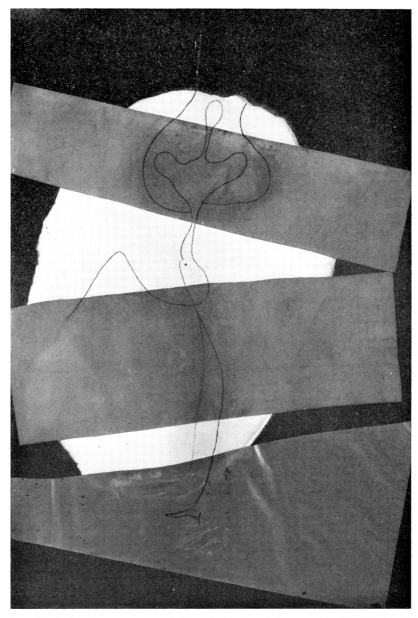

Joan Miró. *La Danseuse*. 1929. Collage (mixed media), 39 × 27 in. The Joseph H. Hirshhorn Collection

Laszlo Moholy-Nagy. *Architecture No. 1.* c. 1920. Oil, 25½ × 21½ in. Private collection, New York

Laszlo Moholy-Nagy. *A II.* 1924. Oil, 45⅝ × 55¾ in. The Solomon R. Guggenheim Museum, New York

Piet Mondrian. *Composition with Colored Planes on White Ground.* 1917. Gouache, 18½ × 23¾ in. Mr. and Mrs. B. H. Friedman

Henry Moore. *Carving*. 1935. Wood, 10½ in.
high, 16 in. long. M. Knoedler & Co., Inc.

Henry Moore. *Figure with Strings*. 1939. Lead, 11 in. long. M. Knoedler & Co., Inc.

Opposite: Henry Moore. *Three-Piece Carving*. 1935. Ebony, 11 × 17 in., including base. M. Knoedler & Co., Inc.

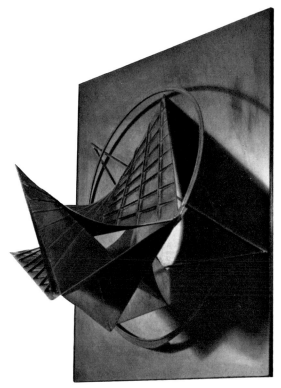

Antoine Pevsner. *Lines and Tangents.* 1934–35. Oxidized brass and copper on plastic, 27⅞ × 25⅛ in. Private collection, New York

Antoine Pevsner. *Figure.* 1925. Copper, 20½ in. high. Mrs. Barnett Malbin (The Lydia and Harry Lewis Winston Collection)

Yves Tanguy. *Shadow Country*. 1927. Oil, 39 × 31⅝ in. Mrs. Barnett Malbin (The Lydia and Harry Lewis Winston Collection)

Yves Tanguy. *With my Shadow*. 1928. Oil, 45⅛ × 32⅛ in. Mrs. Pierre Matisse

Georges Vantongerloo. *Construction of Volume Relations*. 1921. Mahogany, 16⅛ in. high. Collection, The Museum of Modern Art, New York. Gift of Miss Silvia Pizitz

Bram van Velde. *Composition.* 1939. Gouache, 58¼ × 53⁹⁄₁₆ in. Michel Guy